fresh from the farmer's market

summer

fresh from the farmer's market

summer

RYLAND
PETERS
& SMALL

cooking with Alastair Hendy

photography by David Loftus

First published in Great Britain in 1999
by Ryland Peters & Small
Cavendish House,
51–55 Mortimer Street,
London W1N 7TD

Printed and bound in China

ISBN 1 900518 91 0

A CIP record for this book is available from the
British Library

Acknowledgements
My thanks to Egg, of Kinnerton Street, Belgravia,
in London, who were so generous in lending
beautiful bowls for photography, and Kara Kara,
of Tokyo and Pond Place, South Kensington in
London, for Japanese ceramics and other props.
Thanks also to Cityherbs of New Spitalfields
Market, London, for their useful information and
high-quality produce, and to Rebecca Hoyes and
Alasdair Parker for lending us their kitchen and
garden for photography.

Notes
All spoon measurements are level unless
specified otherwise.
Ovens should be preheated to the specified
temperature. If using a convection oven, cooking
times should be reduced according to the
manufacturer's instructions.
Do not serve uncooked or partially cooked eggs
to the very old, very young, or pregnant women.
Specialist Asian ingredients are available in large
supermarkets, Thai, Chinese, Japanese, and
Vietnamese shops, as well as Asian stores.

Designer
Robin Rout
Editor
Elsa Petersen-Schepelern
Editorial Assistant
Maddalena Bastianelli
Publishing Director
Anne Ryland
Production
Patricia Harrington

Food Stylist
Alastair Hendy
Cooking Assistant
Kate Habershon
Stylist
Alastair Hendy
Author Photograph
David Loftus

contents

Red tomatoes, purple eggplants, yellow corn, blueberries, and white peaches are summer's primary colors, the season's culinary building blocks. Simple foods full of vibrant flavor, ripe for endless ideas, they are nature's perfect packages, all perfectly nutritious and perfectly delicious. Mixed with other fresh ingredients, their flavors dazzle and shine. A sun-ripened tomato can be enjoyed draped over garlic-rubbed toast with a dusting of sea salt, pepper, and good splash of olive oil. Or a sunny cob of corn smothered with melting salty butter and masses of freshly crushed black pepper—the more the better. Sugar-dusted berries with a spoon of mascarpone. A perfectly ripe peach, saturated with flavor, just as it is—as nature intended. No knives, no forks, just fingers.

I've kept things simple and to the point. While shopping for ingredients for this book I had to make changes according to what I could find and was at the peak of freshness, so do the same when shopping for my recipes. Change a vegetable or two, according to what you find—if something you see looks really good, buy it, and work it in somewhere.

Nothing is written in stone—your adaptation may work better than mine. It's an instinctual thing. There are lots of serving ideas in this book, but you don't have to present the food the way I have. It all tastes good, and that's what real food is all about. That's the point.

I haven't filled these pages with leafy salads. Though it's summer and the accent on eating is light, we all have our favorite salad ingredients—and the best salads have simple dressings.

So enjoy summer with the recipes and ideas enclosed. Eat outside in the garden or on the veranda or porch. Or pack a picnic and go for the great outdoors. Anywhere, any way, with fresh ingredients like these, your food will taste wonderful.

7

Finding a tomato that tastes like a tomato is difficult these days. Out of season, it's impossible. In season, and grown on home soil, enriched with summer sun, they should taste sweet yet sharp and be densely fleshed with heady scent and a liquid nectar center. Smell and texture, for me, are all part of a good tomato experience. So stick to summer, check their origin, sniff them out, literally.
Don't be seduced by perfection. Blemishes and quirky shapes are the true nature of tomato taste. Plum tomatoes are a good example. When they first appeared in supermarkets they used to look like proper plum tomatoes, like the ones piled high in Mediterranean markets—glowing, gnarled, and fattened, full of sun concentrate and charm. Now, they've often been genetically modified or bred into wishy-washy regularity and a pale imitation of their former selves—you'll get more flavor from a can of good plum tomatoes.
But there is light at the end of the tunnel. For salads, forget the big tomatoes and opt for the babies. Baby ones, on or off the vine, and labeled as "cherry tomatoes" are best. And there are baby plum tomatoes too, deep scarlet globes of true "plum" deliciousness; perfect when briefly roasted in a hot oven with a drop of olive oil, and tossed with basil leaves, sea salt, and black pepper, then served as a salad or piled onto toast. No fancy business—let the tomato flavor shine through. Good tomatoes don't need fuss.
And before I forget, don't keep your tomatoes in the fridge with the rest of the salad ingredients. Try to keep them at their natural temperature (over 50°F)—cold ruins their flavor and there's nothing worse than eating a chilled tomato.
We've all got our favorite ways with this fruit (strange to think of it that way), but here, in case you're wondering what you might do next, are a few more…

matoes

Tomato and pepper soup

with eggplant croutons

It's important to use good, well-flavored tomatoes for this soup—use Italian plum or the so called "vine-ripened" varieties. Water is used instead of stock, to keep the flavors clean and sharp—perfect for the strict non-meat eaters.

4 large red bell peppers, preferably the long, tapered Italian variety

5 tablespoons olive oil

1 large onion, chopped

2 garlic cloves, halved

2 lb. tomatoes, chopped

leaves and stalks from 6 sprigs fresh cilantro (preferably with roots) or basil

a pinch of sugar

1 teaspoon Tabasco (optional)

1 eggplant, quartered lengthwise, inner flesh discarded, flesh cut into small cubes

salt and freshly ground black pepper

Serves 4

1

Put the bell peppers directly on the gas flame of your stovetop. Turn every minute or so until blackened and blistered all over. Alternatively roast them in a preheated oven at 425°F for about 20 minutes. Put them in a covered bowl and let cool. Scrape off the charred peel, then core and seed the flesh.

2

Heat 2 tablespoons of the olive oil in a skillet, add the onion and garlic, and sauté until softened and transparent. Add the peppers, tomatoes, herb stalks, sugar, salt, and pepper. Stew gently for 20 minutes, add 1¾ cups water, and stew for a further 20 minutes.

3

Strain the mixture into a clean saucepan, pushing through all the flesh, and discarding the peel and seeds. Add the Tabasco, if using, warm through (but don't boil), then serve.

4

Season the eggplant then heat the remaining oil in the skillet. Add the eggplant and sauté until golden. Add to the bowls of soup and top with cilantro or basil leaves.

Variations:

• Add chopped black olives and basil or avocado, or sautéed zucchini, sautéed calamari, or feta cheese at the same time as the eggplant.
• Alternatively, omit the peppers from the recipe and serve the soup chilled with a Bloody Mary salsa (chopped avocado, tomatoes, and cilantro, with minced red onion, lime juice, and vodka.)

Roasted tomatoes in herb oil

with char-grilled bread and baby mozzarella

I love it when restaurants give you a bowl of olive oil and balsamic vinegar plus bread and a few olives—just to keep your stomach occupied while you make a decision over the menu. It looks good, needs virtually no preparation, and tastes great—so why not do it at home. Keep it as simple as that, or add sliced tomato and a few basil leaves, or do a little extra preparation, and try this idea—dishes to dip into or pile onto char-grilled bread—a self-assembly toast. This barely needs a recipe.

8 small to medium tomatoes

2–4 tablespoons chopped herbs, such as basil, dill, parsley, oregano, marjoram, and/or chives

2 tablespoons extra virgin olive oil

1 ciabatta loaf, sliced

1 fat garlic clove, halved

1 teaspoon balsamic vinegar

4 baby rounds of fresh mozzarella or 1 large round mozzarella, cut into chunks

sea salt flakes and coarsely crushed black pepper

Serves 4

1

Roast the tomatoes in a preheated oven at 425ºF for about 8 minutes. Cool, peel, and put in a bowl.

2

Mix the herbs with the oil, pour over the tomatoes, and let stand for a few hours or overnight.

3

When ready to serve, char-grill the slices of bread on both sides, then rub with the cut garlic clove. Put the sea salt and pepper in separate small dishes.

4

Drain the tomatoes and reserve the oil. Put the tomatoes in a small dish and strain the oil into another, adding a splash of balsamic vinegar. Add a small dish of the mozzarella.

5

Make up your own toast at the table, or eat the tomato and mozzarella separately and dip the toast in the balsamic oil.

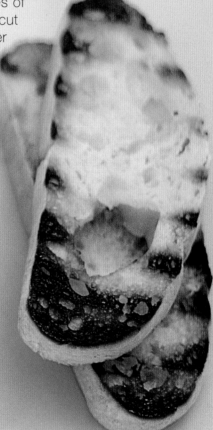

Variations:

• Add extra dishes, such as jars of vegetable antipasto and cured meats from a gourmet store.
• Serve other dishes such as salami, prosciutto, semi-dried tomatoes (page 22), roasted vine tomatoes and bean salad (page 14), or char-grilled eggplant (page 51).

Roasted vine tomatoes

with cannellini bean salad and tapenade oil

Tomatoes grow on bushes, not vines, yet we call tomatoes sold on the stem "vine tomatoes," probably because they look vaguely like a bunch of grapes. Roasted on their stems, they keep that just-picked look on the plate.

4 "vines" of baby tomatoes, about 6 fruit each

extra virgin olive oil, for brushing and dressing

14 oz. canned cannellini beans, rinsed and drained

½ red onion, finely chopped

1 garlic clove, crushed

2 tablespoons coarsely chopped flat-leaf parsley or torn basil leaves

1 tablespoon ready-made tapenade*

½ teaspoon sugar

juice of ½ lemon

sea salt and cracked black pepper

Serves 4

*Tapanade, or olive paste, is available in Italian gourmet stores and larger supermarkets.

1

Arrange the tomato "vines" in a single layer on a baking tray, brush with olive oil, and sprinkle with salt and pepper. Roast in a preheated oven at 425°F for about 6–8 minutes, until the peel has lightly blistered.

2

Put the beans, onion, garlic, parsley, and tapenade in a bowl and stir gently. Dissolve the sugar in the lemon juice and add to the bean mixture. Stir in about 2 tablespoons olive oil and let stand at room temperature for 30 minutes.

3

To serve, spread the bean salad over serving plates, add a "vine" of tomatoes to each plate, spoon over any remaining bean dressing and tomato roasting juices, and dress liberally with more olive oil.

Variations:

• Make into a more substantial course by adding flakes of blackened salmon (page 22), roasted cod, sautéed mullet, or barbecued monkfish kebobs.
• Give it the niçoise treatment and mix the tapenade with mayonnaise, add halved hard-cooked eggs, anchovies, and rare-roasted tuna.

Tomato and bell pepper tart

Use red bell peppers with red cherry tomatoes and yellow peppers with yellow cherry tomatoes. If you prefer, you can also make this tart with tomatoes only (buy 2 baskets extra). Yogurt cheese needs a bit of planning and a square of cheesecloth (this quantity of yogurt makes more than you'll need for this tart—use the rest on toast or with cheese crackers). If you don't have time to make your own cheese, use soft cream cheese instead.

2 cups plain yogurt

1 teaspoon salt

1 large garlic clove, crushed

3 tablespoons finely chopped mixed fresh herbs, such as parsley, basil, chives, dill, and tarragon, plus sprigs for serving

½ package frozen puff pastry (8 oz.), thawed

1 basket cherry tomatoes (about 20)

3 canned red bell peppers or pimientos, drained, seeded, and sliced lengthwise

1 egg, lightly beaten, to glaze

Serves 4

Variations:

• Spread the pastry with a layer of tapenade and top with tomatoes.
• Cover with sliced tomatoes, bake, and serve with fresh pesto.
• Flavor the yogurt cheese with toasted cumin seeds, sprinkle with paprika, and eat with toast.

1

Two days in advance, mix the yogurt, salt, and garlic in a small bowl or pitcher. Place a large square of cheesecloth into a large bowl and pour in the yogurt mixture. Gather up the corners and sides and tie tightly with string. Tie the bundle to a long-handled spoon and suspend over a deep container. Chill for 2 days to allow the whey to drain from the yogurt.

2

When ready to cook, discard the whey, put the yogurt cheese into a bowl and mix in the chopped herbs.

3

Roll out the pastry to a rectangle or circle and spread with half the cheese, leaving a ½-inch border around the edges. Top with the whole baby tomatoes and strips of peppers or pimiento. Brush the edges of the pastry with beaten egg.

4

Bake in a preheated oven at 425°F for 35 minutes or until the pastry has risen and is golden. Sprinkle with herb sprigs and serve hot.

Summer pasta

This isn't a regular baked lasagne: it's much lighter, like a dressed summer pasta—a light and fruity tomato salsa with zucchini and basil, under a blanket of ricotta and pasta.

6 sprigs of basil

5 tablespoons fruity extra virgin olive oil

2 strips of lemon peel

2 strips of orange peel

1 lb. ripe red tomatoes, peeled, seeded, and chopped*

2 sun-dried tomato halves (in oil), very finely sliced

6 baby globe zucchini, halved, or 2 regular zucchini, halved, thickly sliced, then blanched in salted boiling water

1½ cups ricotta, at room temperature

12 sheets lasagne pasta, spinach or plain

salt and freshly ground black pepper

Serves 4

1

Remove the basil leaves from the stems and reserve. Tear up half the leaves and keep the remainder whole. Warm the oil in a small saucepan with the basil stems and citrus peel. Remove and discard the stems and peel.

2

Add the tomatoes, sun-dried tomatoes, salt, and pepper to the oil, then stir in the zucchini. Heat gently for 1 minute. Stir in the chopped basil just before serving. Season the ricotta.

3

Cook the lasagne in a wide saucepan of salted boiling water until just soft—move and separate the sheets as they cook. (You will need 12 sheets, but some may tear or stick together.) Carefully drain the lasagne, then hang the sheets around the edges of the colander so they don't stick together.

4

To assemble the lasagne, make free-form layers of all the ingredients on each serving plate, dress with any remaining infused oil, and sprinkle with salt and freshly ground pepper.

***Note:** Prick the tomatoes all over, put in a bowl and cover with boiling water for 2 minutes. Drain. The peel will slip off easily.*

Variations:

• Use roasted vine cherry tomatoes instead of chopped tomatoes (page 14).

Green tomato and basil curry

This is a thin, soup-like curry. The sharpness of the tart green tomatoes is perfect with the sweet and salt flavors of the curry. If green tomatoes are unavailable, use underripe ones instead, adding them to the pan about 5 minutes before the end of cooking.

1½ lb. green tomatoes, quartered

a handful of basil leaves, chopped, plus extra for serving

5 tablespoons extra virgin olive oil

1¾ cups canned coconut milk

½ tablespoon fish sauce*

2 teaspoons sugar

salt and freshly ground black pepper

Curry paste:

4 large mild green chiles, chopped

5 hot green chiles, chopped

5 shallots, chopped

5 garlic cloves

1½ inches fresh ginger, chopped

1 stalk lemongrass, trimmed, outer casing discarded, chopped

6 kaffir lime leaves*, finely chopped, or 1 teaspoon finely chopped lime zest

2 teaspoons shrimp paste (*blachan*)*, or anchovy essence

Serves 4

1

Put all the ingredients for the curry paste into a food processor or blender and work to a paste. Add 2 of the quartered tomatoes and purée again.

2

Mix the chopped basil in a bowl with 3 tablespoons of the olive oil.

3

Heat the remaining oil in a wok or wide, shallow saucepan, add the paste, and stir-fry until the oil separates—about 4 minutes.

4

Add the coconut milk, fish sauce, sugar, salt, pepper, and 1¼ cups water. Bring to a boil, reduce the heat, and simmer for about 15 minutes. Add the tomato quarters and gently simmer for a further 10 minutes. Stir in the basil-flavored oil and serve with whole basil leaves on top—and plenty of plain boiled rice.

Variations:

• Before serving, you could stir in some fresh pesto, made without Parmesan—the creamy pine nuts add an extra dimension to the taste and texture, not dissimilar to the crushed nuts used in many Asian curry pastes.
• Other possible additions include thin strips of stir-fried beef or chicken and other vegetables, such as Thai wing beans or dwarf beans. Use cilantro instead of basil.
• Bake a red tomato curry using red tomato and red chiles instead of green, adding whole cherry tomatoes 5 minutes before the end of cooking.

Note: *Available at Asian specialty markets. Shrimp paste is a salty Indonesian seasoning. If unavailable, omit it or use anchovy essence.*

Blackened salmon
with semi-dried tomato salad

I like my salmon undercooked. Opaque, moist, and succulent. And this is it—perfect salmon in a matter of minutes. Serve it warm or at room temperature. Semi-dried tomatoes taste like a cross between roasted and sun-dried tomatoes; the slow drying process concentrates the tomato taste and much improves fresh tomatoes low on flavor.

8 plum tomatoes, quartered

4 teaspoons dried oregano

1¼ lb. thick salmon fillet, skin on

1 teaspoon paprika

1 garlic clove, crushed

sea salt and freshly ground black pepper

olive oil, for brushing

Dressing:

4 tablespoons extra virgin olive oil

1 teaspoon balsamic vinegar

Serves 4

1

Put the quartered tomatoes on a baking tray lined with parchment paper. Sprinkle with half the oregano, salt, and pepper, and brush with olive oil. Put onto the bottom shelf of the oven and set to 200°F. Let dry in the oven for 2–3 hours. Check them occasionally in case they dry too fast.

2

Rub the flesh side of the salmon fillet with the remaining oregano, paprika, garlic, salt, and pepper, and then brush all over with olive oil.

3

Heat a heavy, iron skillet (preferably non-stick) until smoking hot. Add the salmon, flesh side down, and sear without moving it for 2 minutes. Turn it over (it should look blackened) and cook for a further 3 minutes; it should be rare in the middle. Remove the skin and flake the flesh into large chunks.

4

To serve, put the flaked salmon and the oven-dried tomatoes on 4 plates. Mix the dressing ingredients together and sprinkle over each serving.

Variations:

• Add torn lettuce leaves, such as batavia (escarole) or romaine, chopped avocado, and fine beans.
• Serve with the tapenade cannellini beans (page 14).
• Use semi-dried tomatoes with broiled vegetables and basil to make a ratatouille salad, or use them in eggplant mozzarella lasagne (page 47).

Corn, believe it or not, makes our world go round. We consume it without knowing it. Most of the world's crop goes into products that shape our everyday lives from toothpaste to tablets, from detergents and paper to glue. It's used to stabilize and add body to processed and canned foods, and to assist pourability—coating sugars and grains so they flow readily. Next time you dust your cookies with confectioner's sugar or refill the salt shaker, think about it.

But it's the fresh corn cob, jammed with sweet summer kernels, that inspires the cook and holds the most dynamic flavor. Corn, maize, sweetcorn (call it what you will) is the outsized fruit of an outsized grass with an exceptionally vibrant taste—sweet, smooth, and warm all at the same time. It's good on its own, picked straight from the plant and eaten immediately, raw—the sugars have had no time to turn to starch, so it's very tender and sweet. Baby corn or candle corn is another variety, bred in an attempt to bring corn down to an acceptable color and polite size—a pale imitation of the parent's fuller figure and flavor. Not good. Sweetcorn is the variety grown to be eaten fresh, but there are others. Dent corn has a starchy kernel and is ground to make cornmeal and polenta (made from soft dent); flint has hard hulls and is used for polenta; popcorn has a very hard husk that pops when heat is applied and the starch within expands dramatically; and a variety that's grown just to make flour, masa, used to make tortillas and tamales. Some of the best recipes for corn come from America, its homeland—thick fish chowders, familiar johnnycakes, breakfast grits, and bean stews like succotash.

"Corn on the cob" is this vegetable's signature dish—the one we all know and love. You can't beat it, boiled or barbecued, with lots of melted butter and freshly cracked black pepper. I tend to get carried away with the pepper mill and am a bit excessive with the butter. But that's what corn on the cob is there for, isn't it? Remember—don't salt the cooking water—this will toughen the kernels; just salt them before serving. And if you feel the cobs are too big, cut them into sections. The jolly giant grass with golden fruit makes far more than a bowl of cornflakes. It's big and bright and always steals the show. So let it.

corn

Char-grilled corn

with chipotle chile butter and cracked black pepper

Chipotles—dried, smoked jalapeño chiles—are the aristocrats of the chile world, with wonderful, complex flavor from the hickory wood used for smoking. Chiles are one of the glories of Mexican cooking and form the perfect marriage with that other New World ingredient, corn.

4 chipotle chiles or other mild dried chiles
or 2 small fresh red chiles, very finely chopped

1 stick butter, at room temperature

½ teaspoon freshly ground cumin

1 teaspoon dried oregano

4 fresh corn cobs

salt and plenty freshly ground black pepper

Serves 4

1

If using dried chiles, soak them in warm water for 20 minutes before using. When soft, split open, discard the seeds, and chop the flesh finely.

2

Mash the butter with the chile, cumin, and oregano.

3

Cook the corn in boiling water for about 8 minutes, then drain. Heat a stove-top grill pan or barbecue until very hot, then cook the corn on all sides until flecked with black.

4

Rub with a generous amount of the chile butter, sprinkle with salt and plenty of pepper, and serve.

Corn and sweet potato bhajia
with hot and sour sambal

Bhajia are delicious vegetable fritters from Indonesia and India. Don't be put off by the long list of ingredients—everything is easily put together. Sambal isn't compulsory, but it's delicious and contains all the flavors of Indonesian cooking, salt, hot, sour, and sweet (you could always use soy sauce instead).

2 fresh corn cobs

1 sweet potato, finely sliced or grated

⅔ cup all-purpose flour

4 small shallots, finely sliced

12 scallions, finely sliced lengthwise

3 tablespoons chopped fresh cilantro

1½ inches fresh ginger, grated

1 garlic clove, crushed

2 small red chiles

1 teaspoon sugar

vegetable oil, for frying

Sambal:

1 stalk lemongrass, trimmed and finely chopped

1 garlic clove, crushed

3 red chiles, finely sliced

1 teaspoon shrimp paste (*blachan*)*, (optional)

1 tablespoon peanut oil

3 teaspoons sugar

4 tomatoes, seeded and chopped

2 tablespoons *kecap manis* (Indonesian ketchup)*
or dark soy sauce

1 tablespoon tamarind paste* mixed with 3 tablespoons water
or 2 tablespoons lime juice with 2 tablespoons water

1 tablespoon crushed toasted peanuts, to serve (optional)

Serves 4

1

To make the sambal, mix the lemongrass, with the garlic, chiles, and shrimp paste and sauté in the peanut oil for about 1 minute. Stir in ½ cup warm water and the remaining ingredients (except the toasted peanuts, if using), let cool, then sprinkle with the peanuts.

2

Meanwhile, to make the bhajia, first cook the corn in a large saucepan of boiling water for 8 minutes. Drain, then hold the corn vertically on a board and slice off the kernels. Discard the core.

3

Mix the corn, sweet potato, flour, shallots, scallions, cilantro, ginger, garlic, chiles, and sugar in a bowl to form a thick batter.

4

Heat the oil in a large skillet, add tablespoons of the mixture and sauté in small batches until golden on both sides. Drain on crumpled paper towels. Serve the bhajia with a small dish of the sambal.

__Note:__ Available at Asian specialty markets.

Corn congee

with vinegared crab, ginger, and crisp glass noodles

Congee is a thick rice soup, popular throughout Asia, and has all sorts of things served with it and in it to pep it up, depending on the time of day it is eaten. It's the muddled balance of all these that makes congee taste good.

2 cups short grain rice, soaked for at least 2 hours

2 quarts light chicken stock

1 teaspoon salt

½ cup cooked corn kernels

8 oz. cooked crabmeat

4 oz. glass noodles (beanthread vermicelli)

peanut or corn oil, for frying

Dressing:

3 tablespoons rice vinegar

2 tablespoons rice wine or mirin (sweetened rice wine)

2 teaspoons sugar

1 small red chile, finely sliced

½ teaspoon salt or 1 tablespoon fish sauce*

Serves 4

To serve (optional):

your choice of: fish sauce*, soy sauce, fresh cilantro, 1 inch fresh ginger, finely grated, poached chicken, chopped fresh shrimp, dried shrimp, or sliced barbecued Chinese pork

*****Note:*** *Available at Asian specialty markets.*

1

Put the rice, chicken stock, and salt in a saucepan and bring to a boil. Reduce the heat and simmer for 1 hour or until the grains have disintegrated. Add some boiling water if the soup becomes too thick. Taste and adjust the seasoning. Add the corn and cook for a further 10 minutes.

2

To make the dressing, mix the rice vinegar, rice wine, sugar, chile, and salt or fish sauce in a bowl and stir until the sugar has dissolved, then use one-third of the mixture to dress the crab.

3

Heat 2 tablespoons of oil in a wok or skillet, add the glass noodles straight from the package, and fry for a few seconds until they become puffy and crisp.

4

Serve the congee in 4 rice bowls set on 4 large plates. Divide the crab between the plates. Serve with the noodles and separate bowls of your choice of the fish sauce, soy sauce, cilantro, ginger, chicken, fresh or dried shrimp, pork, and remaining dressing, all in separate bowls, adding different condiments to your spoon with every mouthful.

Seafood and corn gumbo

Gumbo is the Louisiana classic thickened with filé (ground sassafras leaves) or chopped okra and usually made with seafood, although chicken, duck, and boudin sausage can be used too. My version is more like a *marinière* (no self-respecting Louisiana cook would add wine)—but it tastes wonderful anyway.

1½ lb. mixed seafood, such as mussels or clams, calamari, shrimp, or lobster

1 fresh corn cob

3 tablespoons olive oil

½ teaspoon chile flakes

3 garlic cloves, crushed

3 shallots, chopped

2 carrots, diced

2 teaspoons coriander seeds

¾ cup white wine

1¾ cups chicken stock

juice of 1 lime

a pinch of saffron

4 tomatoes, quartered

7 oz. okra

1 tablespoon chopped parsley

1 tablespoon chopped thyme

sea salt and freshly ground black pepper

To serve:

fresh cilantro sprigs

char-grilled bread or boiled rice

Serves 4

1

Scrub the mussels or clams and discard any that remain open.

2

Boil the corn in unsalted water for about 8 minutes and either cut into chunks or slice the kernels off the cob.

3

Put the calamari, shrimp, if using, and 1 tablespoon of the oil in a bowl with the chile flakes, salt, pepper, and half the garlic. Heat a skillet until smoking hot and sear the calamari and shrimp or lobster for 1 minute. Remove from the skillet and set aside.

4

Heat the remaining oil in the skillet, add the shallots, carrots, coriander seeds, and remaining garlic and sauté until softened but not browned. Add the wine, stock, lime juice, and saffron and simmer for 5 minutes. Add the mussels or clams, corn, tomatoes, and okra and simmer gently for a further 5 minutes. Add the remaining seafood, parsley, and thyme, then taste and adjust the seasoning. Cook for a further 2 minutes.

5

Divide the gumbo between 4 heated bowls, top with cilantro, and serve with char-grilled bread or boiled rice.

Crisp golden chicken
stuffed with ham and cheese, served with corn salad

The good thing about this is that the chicken portions can be fried well before they're needed, then heated in the oven until crisp.

4 free-range chicken legs, skinned and boned*

1¾ cups grated mozzarella or mild Monterey Jack

4 thin slices cooked ham

all-purpose flour, for dusting

1 egg, lightly beaten

6 tablespoons dried or fresh breadcrumbs

2 tablespoons butter

olive oil, for brushing and cooking

salt and freshly ground black pepper

Honey and lime corn salad:

2 fresh corn cobs

½ teaspoon honey

juice of 1 lime

10 cherry tomatoes

6 scallions, halved and finely sliced lengthwise

leaves from small bunch of fresh cilantro, chopped

2 tablespoons sour cream

jalapeño (green) Tabasco, to taste

salt and freshly ground black pepper

Serves 4

Note: To bone the legs, start from the "hip," separating the meat from the bone with the tip of a sharp knife. Follow the bone, keeping the flesh intact until you reach the "knee." Roll back the flesh and carefully scrape the meat from around the cartilage—don't worry about making a few holes. Proceed half way down the next bone, fold back the meat and cut off the bone. A small "handle" of bone will remain. (Your butcher may do this job for you.)

1

To prepare the corn salad, cook the corn cobs for 8 minutes in boiling water. Rub the cobs with olive oil and seasoning and sear in a preheated hot skillet until tinged with a few black speckles. Using a sharp knife, slice the kernels off the cob and reserve.

2

Rub the boned chicken legs inside and out with salt and pepper. Roll the cheese up in the ham and stuff each leg with a ham-cheese roll. Fold over the thigh flap of flesh to enclose the stuffing and secure with a toothpick. Dust each leg with flour, dip into the beaten egg, then roll in the breadcrumbs. Pat on extra crumbs over any bald patches.

3

Heat ⅛ inch depth of olive oil and the butter in an ovenproof skillet and sauté the chicken legs on both sides, about 5 minutes on each side, until golden brown. Transfer to a preheated oven and roast at 375°F for about 15–20 minutes.

4

To complete the salad, dissolve the honey in a bowl with the lime juice, then stir in the corn, tomatoes, scallions, cilantro, sour cream, Tabasco, salt, and pepper. Divide the mixture between 4 plates or bowls, top with the stuffed chicken legs, and serve.

Polenta crust chicken

with avocado corn cream and balsamic-chile dip

Polenta is the Italian version of cornmeal, and also the dish made from it, either a creamy purée or a char-grilled cake. The raw ingredient makes a delicious alternative to a breadcrumb coating, giving a toasted corn flavor to the main dish. Use golden corn-fed chicken to complete the picture.

4 corn-fed chicken breasts, skin on

6 tablespoons instant polenta flour or cornmeal

all-purpose flour, for dusting

1 egg, lightly beaten

vegetable oil, for frying

salt and freshly ground pepper

2 scallions, halved and finely sliced lengthwise, to serve

Avocado corn cream:

1¾ cups cooked corn kernels

4 scallions, chopped

1 garlic clove, crushed

1 small ripe avocado

juice of ½ lemon

1 tablespoon olive oil

salt and freshly ground pepper

Balsamic-chile dip:

2 tablespoons sweet chile sauce

2 tablespoons balsamic vinegar

Serves 4

1

Season the chicken breasts and polenta flour or cornmeal with salt and freshly ground black pepper. Dust the breasts with all-purpose flour, dip in the egg and then roll in the polenta flour (pat on extra if there are any gaps). Chill for 30 minutes.

2

To make the corn cream, put the corn in a food processor and blend to a purée. Add the scallions, garlic, avocado flesh, lemon juice, oil, salt, and pepper and work again to a purée.

3

Mix the chile sauce and balsamic vinegar and put in a small dipping bowl.

4

Heat about ½ inch depth of oil in a large skillet, add the chicken, cover with a lid, and gently sauté for about 6–8 minutes on each side.

5

Slice the chicken into wedges and serve with the avocado corn cream, the balsamic-chile dip, and finely sliced scallion.

Variations:

• Roll up with salad leaves in tortillas.
• Layer into toasted club sandwiches.

37

Eggplants look voluptuous, with nightshade colors and silky sheen lending an air of forbidden fruit. And once they were. They belong to the same family as tomatoes and deadly nightshade, *Solanaceae*, and were thought poisonous. The people of India knew better. They were doing delicious things with them well before the West. We caught on a few hundred years later.

These days, there are many kinds; the familiar large purple, responsible for the European name of "aubergine" (dark purple), the long thin Mediterranean or Asian kinds, the round ones streaked with violet or white, the smooth-skinned white, egg-shaped version. In Thailand, there are even more; small yellow, white, or green and white, with crunch and a slight bitter taste, and sharp-tasting pea eggplants growing in bunches like grapes.

White fleshed and silky smooth when cooked, eggplants absorb oil massively. Like sponges, they will soak up as much as you might care to give them.

There are various approaches to avoid an oil overdose; try cutting them into slices then brushing with oil on both sides before char-grilling or roasting. You can also sauté them in oil, then leave to drain in a colander, or dip the slices in flour and egg before cooking so the batter acts as an oil barrier. Eggplants have little flavor of their own, and this is what makes them so versatile —they readily adopt whatever flavorings you like to add. Try Indian spices, Mediterranean dressings, or Middle Eastern herb mixes.

And finally, to salt or not to salt? Most cookbooks used to advise slicing and salting eggplants before cooking to draw out bitter juices. Large eggplants often do need to be salted, but I think you should leave the Thai ones as they are—they're supposed to be a touch sharp.

plants

Eggplant tempura
with white radish salad and amber dipping sauce

It's a fact—eggplants soak up oil—but dipping slices in batter before cooking will prevent this habit. The eggplant comes out perfectly cooked—soft and melting with a crunchy exterior.

2 eggplants

1 daikon (mooli or white radish), grated, preferably on a mandoline

½ tablespoon black sesame seeds (toasted in a dry skillet)

vegetable oil, for frying

Tempura batter:

2 egg yolks

2 cups ice water

1⅔ cups all-purpose flour (reserve 2 tablespoons for dusting)

1 teaspoon salt

2 teaspoons bonito flakes (optional)*

Amber sauce:

1½ inches fresh ginger, grated then squeezed to extract the juice

3 tablespoons dark soy sauce

3 tablespoons mirin (sweet rice wine)

Serves 4

Note: Sold in Japanese and other Asian stores.

1

Quarter the eggplants lengthwise and cut each quarter in half crosswise. Slice off the core from each piece, leaving a wedge of eggplant about ½-inch thick. Slice "fingers" into each wedge, forming fan shapes.

2

To make the amber dipping sauce, mix the ginger juice, soy sauce, and mirin in a small bowl. Put the daikon in a second bowl and sprinkle with the sesame seeds.

3

Make the batter just before it's needed. Beat the egg yolks with the ice water. Tip the flour, salt, and bonito flakes, if using, into the water mixture and stir briefly—the batter should be lumpy and not properly mixed.

4

Heat the vegetable oil to about 375°F. Dust the eggplant fans with flour, dip into the tempura batter, then straight into the hot oil. Fry until crisp then drain on paper towels. Serve with the white radish salad and the amber dipping sauce.

Variations:

• Fry other vegetables and herbs dipped in batter, for example mint sprigs, zucchini flowers, sweet potato, okra, and shiitake mushrooms and seafood such as sliced fish fillets, whitebait, shrimp, or calamari.

Pea eggplant laksa with shrimp

Pea eggplants, sold in Thai stores, are pea-sized and grow in bunches. They have a tart taste and light crunch. A laksa is a Malay curry with noodles. It can be kept simple with just rice vermicelli noodles and fresh herbs or made more elaborate, by adding seafood, fish cakes, and condiments.

½ cup peanut or corn oil

1 stalk lemongrass, trimmed and smashed

2¾ cups canned coconut milk

3 Japanese eggplants, sliced crosswise

a handful of pea eggplants or peas

6 oz. rice vermicelli noodles

juice of ½ lime

8 large cooked shrimp (optional)

sea salt and freshly ground black pepper

fresh cilantro, to serve

Rempah:

⅓ cup macadamia or cashew nuts

8 small shallots, chopped

4 garlic cloves, crushed

2 small red chiles, chopped

1 inch fresh turmeric root, peeled and chopped (optional)*

1 inch fresh ginger or galangal, chopped

2 teaspoons chopped cilantro root or 1 teaspoon coriander seeds

1 teaspoon shrimp paste (*blachan*)* or anchovy essence

Serves 4

1

Put all the rempah ingredients in a blender or food processor and blend to a paste. Heat the oil in a saucepan or wok, add the paste and stir-fry until darkened. Strain off the excess oil.

2

Add the lemongrass, coconut milk and ¾ cup water. Bring to a fast simmer until reduced and thickened a little. Add the Japanese eggplants and the pea eggplants or peas. Simmer gently for about 10 minutes.

3

Soak the rice noodles in a bowl of hot water until soft—about 15 minutes. Drain and divide between 4 bowls.

4

Season the soup with lime juice, salt, and pepper, then ladle over the noodles. Add plenty of fresh cilantro and 2 shrimp, if using, to each bowl.

Note: Turmeric root is available from Asian markets. It doesn't have a great deal of flavor and is mainly used for its color. The dazzling ocher-colored juices stain everything, including fingers—so handle with care.

Variations:

• Add other cooked seafood such as calamari, octopus, fish pieces, crispy fish cakes, mussels, or clams.

• Other choices are cooked sliced meat or poultry, spicy meat balls, poached egg, other vegetables, crisp shallots, and Asian herbs.

43

Indian pickled eggplant
with egg, basil, and cardamom rice

This pickle has a gently sweet-sour flavor, not sharp. Eat it hot or cold –(it tastes wonderful either way) or serve with freshly baked focaccia instead of rice, and you have great picnic food. Cook ahead, if you can, and leave for a few hours for the flavors to develop and meld—then reheat before serving.

1 inch fresh ginger, chopped

6 garlic cloves

1 onion, chopped

2 medium eggplants, quartered lengthwise, with the central "seed" core removed

½ cup mustard oil, peanut, or corn oil, for sautéing, plus 1 tablespoon extra

2 teaspoons ground cumin

2 teaspoons lightly crushed coriander seeds

3 teaspoons panchphoran spice mix*

a pinch of cayenne pepper

4 tomatoes, chopped

3 tablespoons red wine vinegar

4 teaspoons brown sugar

a handful of fresh basil leaves

8 cardamom pods

2 cups basmati rice

salt and freshly ground black pepper

4 hard-cooked eggs, peeled and halved, to serve

Serves 4

1

Put the ginger, garlic, and onion in a food processor and work to a coarse paste.

2

Sprinkle the eggplants with salt and pepper. Heat ½ cup of the oil in a skillet, add half the cumin and coriander seeds and the eggplant. Sauté on all sides until lightly golden. Put the eggplant in a colander over a bowl.

3

Tip any collected oil from the eggplant back into the skillet, heat, and add the panchphoran. Sauté for a few seconds until the seeds pop. Add the ginger paste, cayenne, and the remaining cumin and coriander seeds and sauté until the oil separates from the mixture, (adding extra oil if necessary). Add the tomatoes, vinegar, and sugar and cook gently for about 10 minutes, stirring occasionally to prevent sticking.

4

Add the fried eggplant to the mixture and cook for a further 5–10 minutes. Add salt and pepper to taste. Keep hot and stir in half the basil just before serving.

5

Heat 1 tablespoon of oil in a deep saucepan, add the cardamom pods, and sauté until aromatic. Add the rice and stir to coat the grains with oil. Add 3 cups water and salt, then cover and bring to a boil. Reduce the heat and simmer very gently for 8 minutes. Turn off the heat and leave covered for 10 minutes.

6

Spoon the rice into 4 heated bowls, then top with the eggplants, the remaining basil, and the halved, hard-cooked eggs.

Variations:

• Use cilantro or mint instead of basil.
• Add fresh curry leaves to flavor the curry or along with the cardamom to flavor the rice.
• Serve the pickled eggplant with pappadams (Indian crispbreads) instead of rice or stir a spoonful of melted creamed coconut into the rice just before serving.

Note: *Panchphoran is available from Indian stores. If you can't find it, make your own: mix 2 teaspoons each of black mustard seeds, cumin seeds, nigella (onion) seeds, fennel seeds, and fenugreek seeds—it's not imperative that you include all of these, but "panch" means "five" in Hindi.*

Eggplant mozzarella lasagne

This is a no-bake lasagne. All you have to do is pre-cook the pasta and vegetables (a few hours in advance, if you like), then quickly assemble all the components, reheat, and serve—a sort of lasagne-in-a-hurry. Fresh and healthy, it looks as if you've spent hours on it.

3 garlic cloves, crushed

1 small bunch of basil, stems and leaves separated

½ cup olive oil

18 sheets lasagne pasta, fresh or dried

2 eggplants, sliced lengthwise into 12 slices

1 tablespoon tapenade or sun-dried tomato paste

3 zucchini (yellow and/or green), thinly sliced lengthwise, then blanched in salted boiling water

1 mozzarella, thinly sliced

salt and freshly ground black pepper

Serves 4

1

Put the garlic, basil stems, and olive oil in a saucepan and warm through for about 10 minutes to infuse the flavors.

2

Cook the lasagne in a wide saucepan of salted boiling water until just soft—move and separate the sheets as they cook. (You will need 12 sheets, but some may tear or stick together.) Carefully drain the lasagne, then put it into cold water to stop it overcooking or sticking together. Hang the sheets around the edges of the colander so they don't stick together.

3

Brush the eggplant slices on both sides with some of the infused oil. Cook in a preheated stove-top grill pan or skillet until seared and soft.

4

To assemble, arrange 4 slices of eggplant across a baking tray. Top each slice with a sheet of lasagne, spread a little tapenade or tomato paste on each, then add a slice of zucchini and mozzarella and a couple of basil leaves. Repeat with all the ingredients, until you have 4 multi-storey piles of pasta, vegetables, and mozzarella. Brush all over with more of the infused oil, cover loosely with foil, and heat through in a preheated oven at 425°F for about 5 minutes or until the cheese begins to melt.

Variations:

• Use semi-dried tomatoes (page 22) instead of sun-dried tomato paste.
• Alternative layering ingredients include goat cheese, Parma ham, soft cheese, toasted pine nuts, cumin seeds, roasted bell peppers, mint, peas, seared scallops, or lemon oil.

Chile lime pan-fried calamari

Thai and violet eggplants with crushed toasted peanuts

Don't give up on the recipe if you can't get the listed eggplants, it will taste very good using ordinary ones. Likewise, use regular limes if kaffirs aren't available. Remember, there are no rules, these recipes are very flexible.

1 lb. prepared calamari (stores can do this for you)

grated zest and juice of 2 kaffir lime* or 1 regular lime

1 tablespoon sugar

1 tablespoon fish sauce*

3 garlic cloves, crushed

1 teaspoon chile flakes

cornstarch, for dusting

12 small Thai eggplants, trimmed and quartered

1 round violet eggplant or small regular eggplant, cut into bite-sized pieces

1 inch fresh ginger, sliced

peanut or corn oil, for sautéing

1 teaspoon *kecap manis* (Indonesian ketchup)* or 2 teaspoons dark soy sauce

To serve:

a few salad leaves

2 tablespoons crushed peanuts, toasted in a dry skillet

Serves 4

Note: *Available at Asian specialty markets.*

1
Slice the calamari into fine rings and separate the ring of tentacles. Put in a bowl and mix in the lime zest and juice, the sugar, fish sauce, garlic, and chile flakes. Let stand for at least 30 minutes.

2
Remove the calamari from the marinade and dust with cornstarch. Add the eggplants and ginger to the marinade and toss well.

3
Heat a shallow pool of oil in a wok or deep skillet. Sauté the calamari in batches for about 1 minute until lightly golden and crisp. Drain on paper towels and keep hot while you cook the remainder.

4
Tip away most of the oil in the wok, leaving about 3–4 tablespoons. Add the eggplant and *kecap manis* or dark soy sauce and stir-fry for 1 minute.

5
To serve, divide the eggplant between 4 plates or bowls, top with the calamari, a few salad leaves, and the crushed toasted peanuts.

Lamb burgers

with char-grilled eggplant, hummus, seed salt, and mint

Homemade burgers are vastly superior to store-bought ones, and so easy to make that we should all make them more often—everyone loves a burger. The seed salt is delicious—store the extra and use it in lots of other ways.

2 tablespoons olive oil, plus extra for brushing

1 onion, finely chopped

2 cloves garlic, crushed

1 small chile, very finely chopped (optional)

1 lb. ground lamb

a handful of mint leaves, chopped, plus extra leaves to serve

1 eggplant, sliced lengthwise

sea salt and freshly ground black pepper

6 oz. hummus, to serve

Seed salt:

1 tablespoon cumin seeds

1 tablespoon sesame seeds

1 tablespoon sea salt

Makes 6 burgers

1

To make the seed salt, toast the cumin seeds and sesame seeds in a dry skillet until the sesame seeds are a light golden brown (watch them, and turn them regularly—they'll burn if left alone). Mix in a bowl with the salt.

2

Heat half the olive oil in the skillet, add the onion, garlic, chile, 2 teaspoons seed salt, and black pepper, and sauté until the onion is soft and transparent.

3

Put the ground lamb in a bowl with the chopped mint, the onion mixture, salt and freshly ground black pepper. Mix well. Shape into burgers, brush with oil, and cook under a hot broiler or in a preheated stove-top grill pan until crisp and brown outside and pink in the middle. Remove and drain on paper towels.

4

Brush the eggplant slices on both sides with the remaining oil and season with salt and pepper. Char-grill on both sides until seared with black lines and softened.

5

Serve the lamb burgers topped with a spoonful of hummus and a fold of eggplant, sprinkled with a little seed salt and a few mint leaves.

Variations:

• To make *baba ganoush*, mash the eggplant with lemon juice, tahini, olive oil, crushed garlic, seed salt, and chopped mint—serve with minted lamb meat balls (use burger mixture).

In the fruit hierarchy, peaches sit at the top of the ladder, deemed the epitome of perfection in the fruit stakes; the "perfect peach," unblemished, velvet-smooth and blushing. It's a shy fruit, serene and understated, with sweet flesh that bruises readily. Bruising attacks the fragile cells within and spreads rapidly—the nectar-like juices turn sour and the flesh turns to mush. Perfection is all, so handle with care!

Ripeness, also, is important—peaches should feel firm with a little give and be faintly scented. Anything vaguely green should be avoided as it will remain rock hard—room temperature will only ripen firm fruit of already peach color. Fruit will be best in peach-growing country, and the longer it stays on the tree before being picked, the better it will taste. From the moment it's picked, it won't get any sweeter. To peel or not to peel? I don't—I'm not into fruit dissection, and it's a fiddly fruit to peel. The warmth of the downy skin against the soft flesh is, to me, all part of the peach-eating experience, and most of the vitamins are stored there. It seems a shame to waste all that goodness and get sticky fingers too. One of the reasons I like peaches so much is that I don't have to peel them. Incidentally, if you want to cut a peach in half to extract the pit neatly, slice around and twist sharply.

The original fruit, a native of China, is still cultivated. It has an outsize pit and very little flesh, but what there is has an unsurpassed taste, and is said to be even better than a white peach. The white peach, I think, is the best variety available, with juicier, more sumptuous flesh than its yellow cousin. But of whatever color, peaches are one of the reasons I most look forward to summer.

aches

Bali duck

and sour peach salad with lime, chile, and nut vinaigrette

This recipe may look like a lot of work, but it's actually a very easy, stress-free process, and Steps 1 and 2 can be done the day before you want to use it. Cooking the duck this way renders the meat succulent and the skin extra crisp, and most of the fat melts away, so it's very healthy too.

1 small duck, about 3 lb.

4 cinnamon sticks, broken

15 cloves, coarsely crushed

4 tablespoons uncooked rice

2 inches fresh ginger, sliced

5 tablespoons brown sugar

kecap manis (Indonesian ketchup)* or dark soy sauce

Sour peach salad:

2 tablespoons peanut oil

4 tablespoons lime or kaffir lime* juice

1 large garlic clove, crushed

1 small red chile, very finely sliced

5 small shallots, sliced lengthwise

2–3 unripe peaches, finely sliced

2 handfuls of bean sprouts, trimmed

a selection of fresh herbs, such as basil, cilantro, or mint

1 tablespoon crushed macadamia nuts or peanuts, lightly toasted

garlic chives or scallions, finely sliced

salt and freshly ground black pepper

Serves 4

Note: Sold in Asian specialty markets.

1

Remove and discard the excess fat from the duck. Pour boiling water over the skin and pat dry with paper towels. Rub the bird with salt and pepper inside and out. Put on a rack in a roasting pan and roast in a preheated oven at 375°F for 1 hour. Remove from the oven, cover loosely with foil, and let cool.

2

Cut the duck into 4 pieces. Line the base of a steamer with a double thickness of foil. Grind 1 cinnamon stick and 3 cloves together and set aside. Mix the remaining cinnamon and cloves with the rice, ginger, and 4 tablespoons sugar. Spread the mixture over the foil. Assemble the steamer and put the roasted duck pieces in the steaming tray, cover, and place over a high heat. When you can smell the aroma of spice, turn the heat to low and let smoke gently for about 20 minutes. Discard the rice mixture.

3

Rub the duck with ½ tablespoon sugar and brush with *kecap manis* or soy sauce and the reserved spices. Put on a baking tray and roast in a preheated oven at 425°F for 20 minutes or until crisp and mahogany brown. Shred the meat from the bone.

4

To make the salad, mix the oil, lime juice, garlic, chile, and the remaining sugar in a large bowl until the sugar has dissolved. Stir in the shallots and 1 teaspoon *kecap manis* or soy sauce. Add the sliced peaches, bean sprouts, herbs, and warm shredded duck and toss well. To serve, pile into bowls and top with toasted crushed nuts and garlic chives.

Squab and peach tagine

Squab are farm-reared pigeons. Their meat is succulent and tender, far superior to wood pigeon. Consequently they're a little expensive and can be difficult to find. Duck breast, guinea fowl pieces, or quail will work just as well, but remember to roast the larger birds for longer, about 20 minutes per pound, while the quail will only need about 8 minutes.

2 squab (French pigeon)

1 teaspoon ground ginger

½ teaspoon ground cinnamon

1 teaspoon ground mace (optional)

olive oil, for brushing and sautéing

3 large onions, finely sliced

3 bay leaves

a pinch of saffron (optional)

10 oz. couscous

chicken stock (see method)

3 garlic cloves, crushed

1 teaspoon paprika

1 teaspoon cumin

1 teaspoon coriander seeds

6 cardamom pods

1 tablespoon pine nuts

2 tablespoons raisins

3 firm peaches, sliced into wedges

sea salt and freshly ground black pepper

Serves 4

1

Rub the squab with salt, pepper, ginger, cinnamon, and mace, if using. Brush with olive oil and put on a baking tray. Roast in a preheated oven at 400°F for 15 minutes. Remove from the oven and let cool.

2

Slice the breast meat and legs from each bird and set aside. Chop up the wings and carcass and put in a saucepan with 3½ cups water. Add half a sliced onion, the bay leaves, salt, and pepper. Bring to a boil, then simmer until reduced to about half volume. Strain and discard all the bones. Add the saffron to the strained stock and infuse for about 10 minutes.

3

Put the couscous in a bowl and pour in the stock until the grains are just covered. Let stand for 5 minutes, then fluff up with a fork. Keep it warm.

4

Heat 3 tablespoons olive oil in a skillet, add the remaining onion and the garlic, and sauté until soft and lightly caramelized. Add all the spices, pine nuts, and raisins and sauté for a few minutes more.

5

Spoon the mixture into a shallow saucepan or skillet with a lid. Pour over the remaining stock. Put a layer of sliced peaches on the top, followed by a layer of squab pieces. Put the lid on the pan or skillet and simmer over a low heat for about 10 minutes.

6

Serve on heated dinner plates with separate bowls of saffron couscous.

Vanilla creamed peaches

with frangipane pastries

For pure peach flavor, purée very ripe peaches with the vanilla seeds and leave out the wine—taste and add enough sugar to suit your mood. You could also poach the peaches whole, then skin them and serve with their juices and the cream. *Frangipane* is an almond-flavored cream.

6 peaches

1 bottle white wine (27 fl. oz.)

⅔ cup sugar

1 vanilla bean, split lengthwise

⅔ cup heavy cream, whipped

Frangipane pastries:

8 oz. puff pastry

7 oz. white marzipan

confectioner's sugar, for rolling

Serves 4

1

Put the peaches in a saucepan with the white wine, sugar, and vanilla bean and bring to a boil. Reduce the heat and simmer for 20 minutes or until the peaches are soft. Remove them from the syrup and let cool.

2

Discard the peel and pits. Put the flesh in a food processor with a drop of the poaching syrup and blend to make a smooth purée. Chill.

3

To make the frangipane pastries, roll out the pastry to about ⅛ inch thick. Dust the work surface with confectioner's sugar and roll out the marzipan as thinly as possible. Lay the pastry over the marzipan, then roll up together to make a long sausage shape. Cut the sausage crosswise into ½-inch thick slices, then roll or press each one into a flattened oval. Arrange on a baking tray and cook in a preheated oven at 350°F for about 15 minutes or until puffed and tinged golden brown.

4

Spoon the creamed peaches into small bowls, streak cream over the top, and serve with the frangipane pastries for dipping.

Variations:

• Spoon the creamed peaches over ice cream.
• Purée with honey and serve with yogurt.
• Churn in an ice cream machine to make sorbet, or mix with the yogurt and freeze to make ice cream.

Peach and fig almond tart

If peaches are the essence of summer, then figs are its very soul. I love the big purple ones and the little green honey-flavored variety. I don't skin them, though many people prefer to—I like their color, especially the purple.

8 sheets phyllo pastry, or enough to make 4 layers

melted butter, for greasing and brushing

1 tablespoon sugar

1 egg, lightly beaten

8 oz. mascarpone

4 tablespoons ground almonds

4 ripe peaches, pitted and sliced

4 figs, halved or quartered

1 tablespoon dark brown sugar, preferably unrefined

Serves 4

Variations:

• Substitute other fruits, such as blueberries and plums, nectarines, or poached pears.

1

Grease a 14 x 4 inch rectangular or 8½ inch circular pie pan and line with a single layer of phyllo pastry (about 2 overlapping sheets). Trim the pastry leaving about ½ inch sticking up above the rim of the pan. Brush with melted butter and line with another 2 sheets of pastry. Repeat until all the pastry has been used.

2

Beat the sugar and egg in a bowl, then beat in the mascarpone and almonds. Spread over the base of the tart.

3

Arrange the pieces of peaches and figs all over the mascarpone cream until the pie shell is full. Sprinkle with the brown sugar and brush more butter over the pastry and fruit.

4

Put on a baking tray and bake on the middle shelf of a preheated oven at 400°F for about 35 minutes or until tinged golden brown.

White peaches in strawberry champagne

The white peach is the queen of peaches and, being a little more expensive than your regular peach, deserves regal treatment. The recipe requires a large number of strawberries, so buy them cheaply at your local market when there's a glut of them at the height of the season. Make sure you cut out any soft bits from the fruit—bad fruit will tarnish the taste.

1
Put the strawberries, sugar, and lemon juice into a large saucepan. Place over the lowest heat possible and gently stew for 1 hour. The process is complete when the fruit has turned to an unattractive gray mush and has exuded all its juice.

2
Line a conical strainer with cheesecloth and place over a saucepan. Tip the contents of the pan into the strainer and leave for 2 hours to let the clear red juices run through. Do not be tempted to squeeze the fruit to extract the last few drops. Alternatively, tie up the cheesecloth into a bag, put a wooden spoon through the knot, and hang it over the pan.

3
Discard the cheesecloth and its contents. Add the champagne to the strawberry juice and warm through over a gentle heat. Add the peaches, let cool, then chill. Serve chilled with heavy cream or crème fraîche.

3 lb. strawberries

3 tablespoons sugar

juice of 1 small lemon

1 bottle champagne or other sparkling wine (28 fl oz.)

1 lb. ripe white peaches, pitted, skinned, and finely sliced

heavy cream, whipped, or crème fraîche, to serve

Serves 4

Variations:
- Instead of the peaches, use sliced nectarines and whole strawberries.
- Serve with chile and kaffir lime ice (page 65).
- To make strawberry champagne jellies, add gelatin (follow package instructions) to the hot strawberry juice, pour into serving bowls, top with peaches, and chill.

62

Broiled peaches with chile kaffir lime ice

Chile and kaffir lime ice is addictive. It may sound strange but it works. The sharp iciness of the lime kicks in first and the chile infusion adds a warming aftertaste. Particularly good with these caramelized peaches.

4 peaches, halved and pitted

2 tablespoons dark brown sugar

1 teaspoon ground allspice

2 tablespoons butter, softened

Kaffir lime ice:

5 limes, preferably kaffir limes*
(grated zest of 2, juice of 5)

3 small hot chiles, split and seeded

2 cups confectioner's sugar, sifted

2 cups crème fraîche

3 tablespoons ice water

Serves 4

Note: Available at Asian specialty markets.

1

To make the ice, put the lime zest and juice, the chiles, and confectioner's sugar in a bowl and mix to dissolve the sugar. Set aside for 30 minutes to develop the flavors.

2

Remove and discard the chiles. Beat the crème fraîche thoroughly into the lime syrup. Spoon into a covered container and freeze—there is no need to stir. Remove from the freezer and leave at room temperature for 10 minutes before serving.

3

Just before serving, sprinkle the peach halves with sugar and allspice, and smear with butter. Lightly brown under a hot broiler. Put half a peach in each bowl and serve with the ice.

Variations:

• For a lighter ice, use whipped heavy cream instead of crème fraîche.
• Serve the ice with sautéed or broiled bananas, or stir through raspberry purée to make a ripple.
• Serve the peaches with crème fraîche beaten with ginger syrup or toasted pine nuts and yogurt.

65

Summertime is berry time. Sweet downy raspberries, over-stuffed strawberries, velvet-bloomed blueberries, tart gooseberries, and sweet beads of white or red currants, all eaten straight from the package. Our favorites are strawberries, sugar-dusted and swimming in cream. But do you hull them first or not? I must admit I don't, but if you do, make sure you do it after they've been washed— otherwise you'll have waterlogged fruit. Soft berries with a bloom, such as raspberries or blueberries, shouldn't be washed as (like mushrooms) this interferes with their fragile epidermal layers and, apart from losing their velvety texture, they can turn to mush.

When buying berries in the supermarket always check under the container and avoid any with excessive juice—easily identifiable through a plastic box. This indicates overripe or bruised fruit. "Pick your own" berries, where you gather fruit straight from the farmer's field, is the surest route to getting the freshest sun-ripened berries, and with no transportation and refrigeration involved, they taste fantastic. (And you can eat for free as you pick.)

Speaking of food for free, at the end of summer you can pick blackberries and elderberries growing wild. They may need sugar as they can be tart, but are particularly good used in pies, jams, or sauces.

Cultivated "wild" foods, from wild arugula to wild mushrooms, are all the rage. And most fashionable of the berry set are wild strawberries (*fraises des bois*), the American ancestor of the regular strawberry. Dainty, fragrant, and oh-so-fragile, they are the caviar of strawberries. Finding them growing wild is now rare but you can buy them from specialty fruit stores. Expensive? Yes. Their shelf life is non-existent and they go mushy very quickly—so eat them the same day.

Hybrids, such as loganberries, youngberries, boysenberries, and tayberries, are the result of crossbreeding raspberries, blackberries, or dewberries. In addition, we have golden raspberries and, if you're lucky, white to pale gold cloudberries, found throughout Scandinavia and around the Arctic Circle. Gosh, it's confusing —I'll think I'll stick to the original, the raspberry, a perfectly happy little chap.

berries

Raspberry ripple

Store-bought ripple is not what it used to be. This one is the real thing and looks the part, with pure vanilla ice cream, streaked with painterly lines of fresh raspberry purée. A classic combination.

2¾ cups milk

1 vanilla bean, split lengthwise

1¼ cups sugar

7 egg yolks

2¾ cups heavy cream, whipped to soft peak stage

Ripple:

8 oz. raspberries, plus extra to serve

5 tablespoons sugar

1 tablespoon lemon juice

Serves 4

1

Put the milk and vanilla bean in a saucepan. Bring to a boil, remove from the heat, and let cool for 30 minutes. Discard the vanilla bean.

2

Beat the sugar and egg yolks in a bowl, then pour in the vanilla milk. Put into a saucepan and heat gently, stirring continuously, until you have a thin custard (too much heat and the custard will curdle and separate). Cool, then chill. Fold the whipped cream into the cold custard, pour into a covered container, then freeze.

3

Put the raspberries, sugar, lemon juice, and 1 tablespoon water into a saucepan, bring to a boil, reduce the heat, and simmer until soft. Push the mixture through a non-metal strainer into a bowl. Chill.

4

Remove the ice cream from the freezer and let soften until spreadable. Spoon one-third of the mixture into a shallow square or rectangular container lined with plastic wrap. Mark parallel uneven furrows in the ice cream, then pipe the raspberry purée into the furrows. Carefully spread over another layer of softened ice cream, repeating until all the ice cream and raspberry mixture has been used. Finish with more wobbly stripes of ripple. Freeze until set.

5

To serve, remove from the container, discard the plastic wrap, and trim the sides straight if necessary. Serve alone or with fresh raspberries.

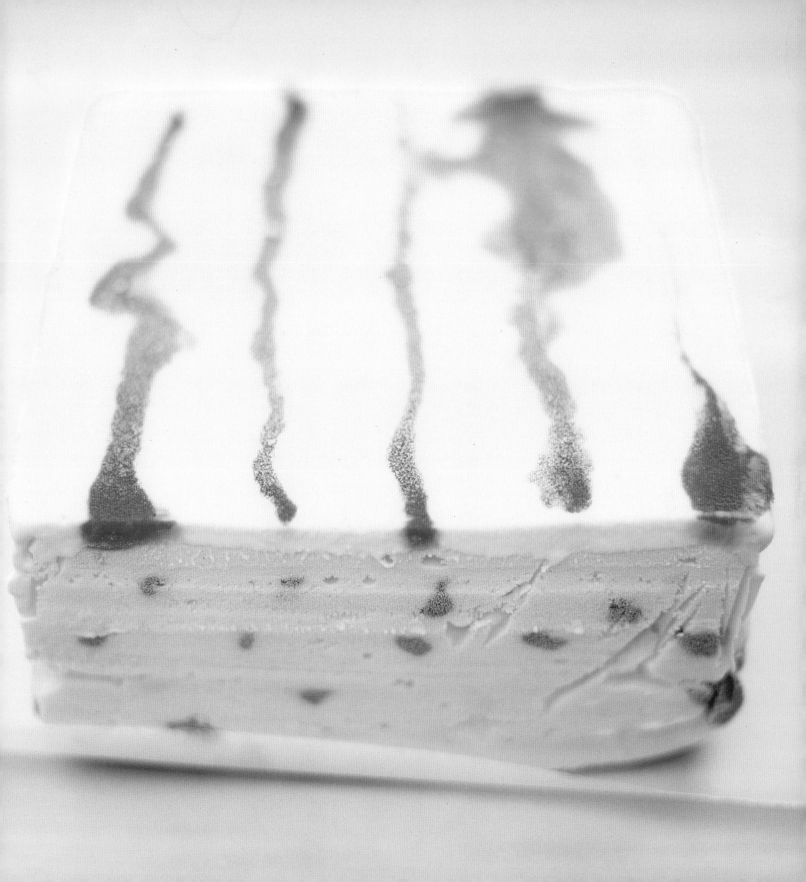

Summer fruit curd

with shortbread cookies and fresh berries

Sharp and sweet berries, a passionfruit and lemon creamed curd, and crumbly shortbread cookies—the perfect finale for lunch at the end a long summer afternoon. If you really want to be lazy, use a jar of quality lemon curd instead—just stir in some passionfruit juice.

Summer fruit curd:

1 stick unsalted butter

1⅓ cups sugar

sieved flesh from 4 passionfruit

3 lemons

3 eggs, beaten

8 oz. mascarpone

Shortbread cookies:

5 tablespoons sugar

1 stick unsalted butter, softened

1 egg yolk

2 teaspoons grated lemon zest

1¼ cups all-purpose flour, sifted

To serve:

4 baskets berries, such as wild strawberries, white, black or red currants, elderberries, raspberries, blackberries, or blueberries, about 1 lb. in total

Makes 8

1

To make the curd, put the butter, sugar, and passionfruit pulp into a heatproof bowl with the juice of 1½ lemons and the grated zest of all 3. Fit the bowl over a saucepan of simmering water (the water should not be in contact with the bowl) and stir the mixture until the butter has melted and the sugar dissolved.

2

Add the beaten eggs and stir until the mixture thickens enough to form a film on the back of a spoon. Don't overheat or the mixture may curdle. Let cool.

3

To make the shortbread, mix the sugar, butter, egg yolk, and lemon zest in a bowl, then work in the flour to form a smooth dough. If it is too sticky, dust with flour, then work in. Chill for 20 minutes, then roll out the dough and cut out disks with a 2-inch cookie cutter. Arrange apart on a baking tray, then bake in a preheated oven at 325°F for 30 minutes. Remove from the oven, let cool on the baking tray for a couple of minutes, then transfer to a wire rack and let cool completely.

4

Beat the curd and mascarpone together until smooth. Serve the curd and berries in separate bowls, accompanied by the cookies. Alternatively, for an ultra-stylish serving idea, cut tracing paper into strips, and wrap each strip around a cookie and secure with tape or string. Fill with fruit curd and top with your choice of berries.

Golden raspberries with clove chocolate

Golden raspberries taste the same as pink raspberries, but I love their color—the honey glow of late summer. The clove truffled chocolate can be served as a slab or cut into small cubes—serve them *en masse* on a length of paper with a pile of wooden disposable forks or bamboo skewers. Alternatively, line up the chocolates in a paper-lined box, add some berries, and present them as a gift.

1

Line a 1¾ inch deep X 7-inch square cake pan with plastic wrap.

2

Put the two chocolates in a heatproof bowl and fit over a saucepan of simmering water (the bowl must not come in contact with the water). Let the chocolate melt.

3

Mix the ground cloves and cream in a bowl. Remove the chocolate from the heat and gently stir the clove cream into the melted chocolate—do not beat. Pour the mixture into the lined container, smooth with a palette knife, and chill until set.

4

When set, use the edges of the plastic wrap to lift the chocolate slab from the container. Invert onto a wooden board and peel away the plastic wrap. Bring to room temperature, then slice into cubes. Dust with cocoa, then serve with the berries.

1¼ lb. plain chocolate, broken into pieces

7 oz. unsweetened chocolate (about 60 percent cocoa solids), broken into pieces

12 cloves, finely ground

3 cups heavy cream

unsweetened cocoa powder, for dusting

2–4 baskets golden raspberries or other berries, about 8 oz. in total

Makes about 36 cubes

Variations:

• Serve sliced fresh figs, candied oranges, or vanilla-poached pears instead of berries.
• Raisins soaked in orange liqueur or orange flower water can be stirred into the chocolate mixture before it sets.

Summer pudding

Traditional English summer pudding, made from melted berries and juice-soaked bread, is delicious, but needs planning, to give it time to saturate and set. This combination of berry juices and strawberries on toast is an instant version—though the fruit mixture will still benefit from being left for a few hours if you have time. It looks just as elegant as the original.

4 baskets mixed berries, such as redcurrants, raspberries, blueberries, and blackberries, about 1 lb.

6 tablespoons sugar

7 oz. strawberries, stems removed and halved

4 slices brioche or white bread

butter, for spreading

To serve:

wild strawberries (optional)

mint leaves

confectioner's sugar, for dusting

thickened heavy cream

Serves 4

1

Pick over the baskets of fruit, removing any stems or leaves. Put the berries in a saucepan with ¼ cup water and the sugar. Bring to a boil, then reduce the heat and simmer gently for about 8 minutes.

2

Put the halved strawberries in a bowl and press the cooked fruit syrup through a non-metal strainer over the strawberries. Let stand for at least 30 minutes, then chill. Alternatively, leave overnight in the refrigerator.

3

When ready to serve, toast the brioche or bread, spread with butter, and spoon the fruit syrup over each slice. Arrange the glazed strawberries over the tops, surround with wild strawberries, if using, and sugar-dusted mint leaves. Serve the cream separately.

Variations:

• You needn't strain the fruit, just pile it all on toast, top with thick cream, and serve.
• Try using warmed doughnuts instead of toast.
• Serve the berry juice and strawberry mixture with vanilla ice cream.

Blueberry cheesecake

Yes, there's a pastry to make, but it's so easy, and rolling it straight onto the pan stops it tearing. Easy to make and light to eat, the filling is virtually fat free and the pastry base is so thin you can have seconds without worrying about calories. The base and filling hold up well if you want to make it in advance—add the fresh fruit just before serving.

10 oz. blueberries

mint leaves

confectioner's sugar, for dusting

heavy cream, to serve (optional)

Pastry base:

5 tablespoons sugar

1 stick unsalted butter, softened

1 egg yolk

1 teaspoon grated lemon zest

1¼ cups all-purpose flour, sifted

Cheesecake filling:

1⅔ cups low-fat soft cheese

4 eggs, yolks and whites separated

1 teaspoon grated lemon zest

⅔ cup sugar

1 tablespoon all-purpose flour

Serves 6–8

1

Butter a 8-inch springform pan and base-line with waxed paper.

2

To prepare the pastry base, mix the sugar, butter, egg yolk, and lemon zest in a bowl. Add the flour and work to a smooth dough. If it is too sticky, dust with flour, then work in. Chill for 20 minutes.

3

Put the base of the springform pan on the work surface and roll out the pastry on top to approximately ⅛-inch thickness. Trim around the base with a knife and discard the excess pastry. Assemble the pan and bake in a preheated oven at 300ºF for 20 minutes until half cooked. Let cool. Reduce the oven temperature to 275ºF.

4

To make the cheesecake filling, mix the cheese in a bowl with the egg yolks and lemon zest. Beat the egg whites until stiff, then gradually beat in the sugar and flour. Fold the egg white mixture into the cheese mixture and spoon over the part-cooked pie shell in the pan. Sprinkle with 2 tablespoons of the berries and bake on the middle shelf of the oven for about 1 hour or until firm to the touch. Let cool.

5

To serve, top with a tumbling pile of the remaining fruit, sprinkle with a few mint leaves, dust with confectioner's sugar, and serve with cream, if using.

Lemongrass yogurt rice

with crushed raspberries

Mix and match the refreshing lemongrass yogurt rice with the sweet crushed fruit as you go—or you could even spoon the berries and juice into the bowls first and cover with the rice, then dig deep for the berries as you eat.

8 oz. raspberries

⅔ cup sugar

1 tablespoon lemon juice

½ cup short-grain rice, washed

4 stalks lemongrass, trimmed and smashed open

3 cups milk

1 lb. creamy yogurt

Serves 4

1

Put half the raspberries in a saucepan and stir in half the sugar and 1 tablespoon water. Bring to a boil, then reduce the heat and simmer until the fruit is soft. Push the fruit and juice through a non-metal strainer into a bowl, discarding the pips. Stir in the lemon juice, then add the remaining raspberries to the purée, crush lightly, and let cool.

2

Put the rice, lemongrass, milk, and the remaining sugar into a saucepan, bring to a boil, stir well, reduce the heat, and simmer for 30 minutes. Let cool, then discard the lemongrass.

3

Stir the yogurt into the lemongrass rice, then divide between 4 bowls and serve with small bowls of crushed raspberries.

Variations:

• Flavor the rice with a split vanilla bean rather than lemongrass and serve with a purée of mixed berries.
• Serve the berries with thick yogurt and honey, sprinkled with toasted slivered almonds.

index